To my Grandad Maurice French
and all the French & Tustain family ♥

Copyright © 2020 by Serena Ferrari
All rights reserved. No part of this book may be reproduced, transmitted or stored in an information retrieval system in whole or in part or by any means, graphic, electronic or mechanical, including photocopying, taping and recording, without prior written permission from the author and publisher.

Author: Serena Lane Ferrari (www.serenalaneferrari.com)
Illustrator: Giorgia Vallicelli (www.giorgiavallicelliart.com)
Published by I love Myself Books

First Printing, 2020
ISBN: 979-12-200-6161-2

The Butterfly Inside

Written by
Serena Lane Ferrari

Illustrated by
Giorgia Vallicelli

Every day, Oliver dreamed of becoming a butterfly, gliding through the air and floating gently on the evening breeze.
But Oliver was no butterfly, he was an Elf and had no wings.

One day, Oliver bumped into a bloom,
a plan flashed in his mind.

"I will find the strongest, most colorful flower petals in the garden. I will make them into wings—butterfly wings—all of my very own!"

Promptly, Oliver began to gather flower petals. They were as soft and smooth as his favorite blanket. Oliver worked all night inside his little mushroom house under the oak tree.

"Mr. Owl!" Oliver exclaimed proudly.
"I am working on my transformation.
Will you carry me to the orchard to find Captain Ant?"
"Hop on my back, Oliver!" said Mr. Owl.

And off they flew.

"Captain Ant, can you help me turn my flower petals into butterfly wings?" asked Oliver.
"Of course, Oliver!" replied Captain Ant.

"I think I know just how to help you.
Ants are pretty good when it comes to making things."
Captain Ant and his troop helped Oliver all morning,
bending flower stems into the shape of wings.

By the end of the day, Oliver had his wings.
They were strong wings.
He tried sticking them on with some snail slime and with tree sap glue.
But nothing worked.

Mr. Crow laughed and laughed.
But Oliver was too determined to listen to a cackling crow.

"Now I need to find Miss Spider," said Oliver.
She weaves such strong webs out of silk.
She could weave the wings on my back.
"Miss Spider, YUHUUUU," he shouted. "Where are you?"
Miss Spider slid down from her web.
"Will you please help me fix my wings to my back?" asked Oliver.

As kind as ever, Miss Spider climbed onto Oliver's creation and carefully wove her silk around the petal wings, fastening them securely to Oliver's back and arms.
"Wow!" said Oliver.
"I have wings! I really look like a butterfly now."

Oliver climbed up the rock and set off to fly, but…

…he tumbled down and banged his head.
This time, Crow had all his friends laughing, too.

Oliver, with a tear rolling over his cheek, got up and tried again.

SPLASH!

"Go and fetch Lady Robin!" said Miss Spider.
"She teaches all her babies to fly."

Lady Robin was busy giving her four little robins flying lessons.
"Good evening, Lady Robin," said Oliver,
"can you please teach ME to fly?"
Lady Robin stared at his wings.

"Dear Oliver, you will have to read the wind,
watch the breeze and follow the air currents.
Then just glide on your wings,
head up and no dangling legs."

Oliver climbed to a lower branch of the tree.
He felt calm and knew he was ready to complete his amazing journey to fly.
All the butterflies in the land gathered above, waiting to welcome their newest member.
"You can do it, Oliver," said Lady Robin.

Oliver took a deep breath.
His heart beat fast, and his cheeks turned pink.
He dove off the branch and swooped like a kite.
"I'm flying! I'm really flying!"

Oliver gently twirled and whirled in the air.
Full of joy, he soared.
Oliver danced in the sky with all the other butterflies.

You can be whatever you dream!

We proudly support

Reforestation is the most
effective method to fight climate change

Serena Lane Ferrari   Giorgia Vallicelli

You buy books, we plant trees.

From the Author

I write books for young children that have the **future of our planet** at their heart. I passionately believe that children are our last chance to improve our ecosystems, find solutions to major climate problems, and save the planet.

I also believe in the importance of **reading to children** from an early age, and hope that my books engage children (and parents!) and inspire them to believe in a better future.

I love hearing from readers, and welcome you to **interact with me** on instagram (www.instagram.com/serenalaneferrari) or to **contact me** at serenalancferrari@gmail.com

Would you mind taking a few seconds to leave a review of my book? It's important because **your opinion** helps people make better decisions.

Thank you!

Serena Lane Ferrari

Sneak Peek

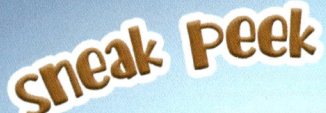

STINKY SUPER SKUNK

Even Stinky's name is stinky! And he's tired of it. Join the Journey of one little skunk who has been given a secret gift from Mother Nature, but doesn't know it yet! When tragedy strikes in the forest, Stinky learns that **being unique has its advantages**. A fun and engaging story about how being different is actually good, even when it starts off feeling bad.

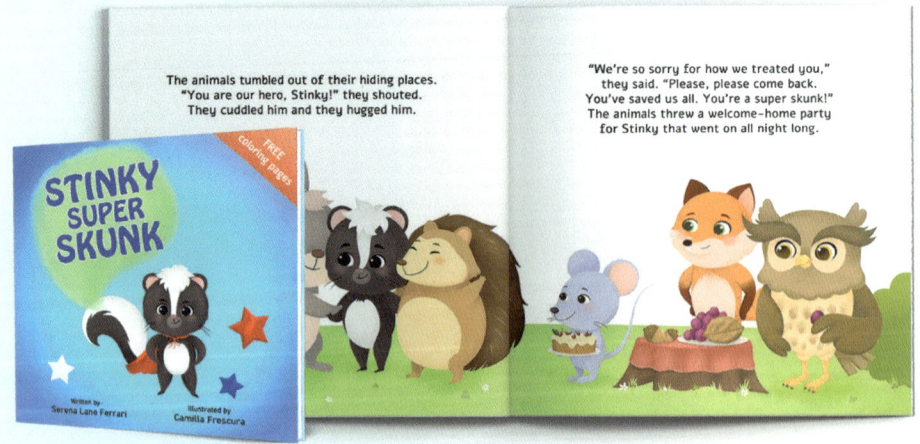

Other Books available:

Did You Steal my MILK?

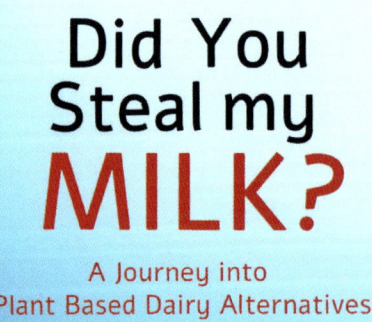

A Journey into Plant Based Dairy Alternatives

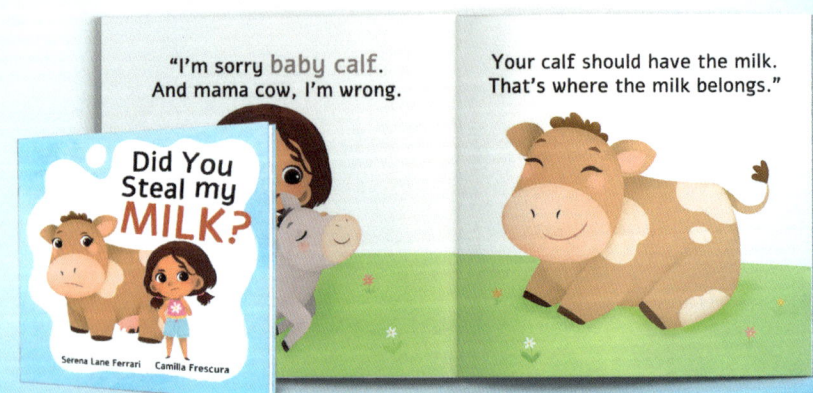

SAVE THE PLANET BOOKS SERIES

Jingo in the Jungle
Saving the Jewels of the Earth

Saving Tally
An Adventure into the Great Pacific Plastic Patch

The Hidden Spaceship
A Journey into Environmental Awareness

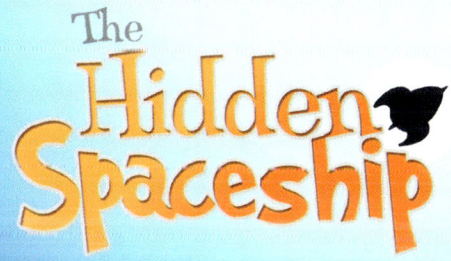

This book was released in April 2020 during a world-wide Covid-19 pandemic.

I hope this book will bring escapism, optimism, and positivity to all the children in the world.

A special thanks to all the doctors, nurses, medical staff and key workers around the globe.

Welcome home to Andrea, Claudio, Clarissa, Loredana, Carolyn and very young Isabella who won their battle against the virus.

Goodbye, Aunt Luisa, you were a great woman. ♥

Printed in Great Britain
by Amazon